UPDATED EDITION

Guess What!

Student's Book 2
with eBook

American English

Susannah Reed with Kay Bentley

Series Editor: Lesley Koustaff

CAMBRIDGE

Contents

3

Hello again!

Look!

1 🎧 0.01 **Listen. Who's speaking?**

2 🎧 0.02 **Listen, point, and say.**

1 Ben
2 Olivia
3 David
4 Tina
5 Leo

3 🎧 0.03 **Listen and find.**

Find Leo

Say the chant.

sister

This is my sister.
Her name's Olivia.
How old is she?
She's eight.

brother

friend

friend

Find the mistakes and say.

Number 1. His name's Ben. He's eight.

1

Name:
David

Age:
6

2

Name:
Tina

Age:
7

3

Name:
Ben

Age:
5

4

Name:
Olivia

Age:
9

6 **Sing the song.**

Happy, happy, look and see,
We can sing our ABCs.

7 **Listen and point.**

Dan   Jill   Sam   Sue   Tom

8  **Ask and answer.**

What's your name?   My name's Harry.

How do you spell "Harry"?   It's H-A-R-R-Y.

Grammar: *Hello. What's your name?*
How do you spell … ?

→ Workbook page 6

9 🎧 0.09 **Listen, look, and say.**

1 What's this?

It's a ruler.

2 What are these?

They're books.

10 🎧 0.10 **Listen and point.**

11 **Ask and answer.**   b, 1. What's this?   It's a red bike.

Grammar: *What's this?*

Grammar fun!

13 Talk Time **Listen and act.**

Animal sounds

14 Listen and say.

The rabbit can run. The lion is lazy!

What kind of **art** is it?

1 🎧 0.16 Listen and say.

photography

drawing

sculpture

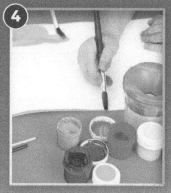
painting

2 CLIL ▶ Watch the video.

3 Look and say the kind of art.

Number 1. Sculpture.   Yes.

Guess What!

Let's collaborate!

ARE WE THE SAME?
compare
discuss
think
ask
talk
answer

① Transportation

Guess What!

15

1 🎧 1.01 **Listen. Who's speaking?**

2 🎧 1.02 **Listen, point, and say.**

1 plane

2 helicopter

3 bus

4 car

5 truck

6 motorcycle

7 train

8 boat

9 tractor

3 🎧 1.03 **Listen and find.**

Find Leo

4 Say the chant.

This is my car.
It's a big, red car.
This is my car,
And it goes like this.
Vroom! Vroom!

bike

train

boat

car

5 Match and say.

Number 1, c. It's a tractor!

1

2

3

4

a

b

c

d

6 Ask and answer.

Do you like motorcycles?   Yes, I do.

7 (1.06) **Sing the song.**

I have a ,
You have a .
He has a ,
And she has a .

Let's play together.
Let's share our toys.
Let's play together.
All the girls and boys.

I have a ,
You have a .
He has a ,
And she has a .

Let's play together ...

I have a ,
You have a .
He has a ,
And she has a .

Let's play together ...

8 (1.07) **Listen and say the name.**   She has a train.   May.

Tim

May

Alex

Lucy

Grammar: *I have a truck.*   → Workbook page 14

9 🎧 1.09 **Listen, look, and say.**

Does he have a plane?

Yes, he does.

Does she have a plane?

No, she doesn't. She has a car.

10 🎧 1.10 **Look and match. Then listen and answer.**

Number 1. Does she have a ball? No, she doesn't.

1 2 3 4 5

a b c d e

11 **Ask and answer.**

Number 1. Does she have a ball? No, she doesn't.

Grammar fun!

 Listen and read. Watch.

13 **Talk Time** **Listen and act.**

Animal sounds

14 **Listen and say.**

A gorilla on the grass. A hippo in the house.

Where is the
transportation?

1 🎧 1.16 Listen and say.

on land

on water

in the air

2 CLIL ▶ Watch the video.

3 Look and say *on land*, *on water*, or *in the air*.

Number 1. On land.   Yes.

Guess What!

Let's collaborate!

OUR ECO-FRIENDLY TRANSPORTATION

ferry

car

draw

invent   choose   bike

2 Pets

Guess What!

theme

25

1 🎧 2.01 **Listen. Who's speaking?**

2 🎧 2.02 **Listen, point, and say.**

1 woman

2 man

Pet Show

3 girl

4 cat

5 mouse

6 fish

7 boy

8 dog

9 baby

10 frog

3 🎧 2.03 **Listen and find.**

Find Leo

4 🎧 2.04 Say the chant.

mice

One frog, two frogs.
Big and small.
Come on now, let's count them all.
One, two, three.
Three green frogs.

fish

dogs

frogs

5 Look, find, and count. I can see two women.

women

men

babies

children

6 🔵 Look at your classroom. Then say. I can see five boys.

7 🎧 2.06 **Listen, look, and say.**

1
beautiful

2 ugly

3
old

4
young

5 happy

6 sad

7 big

8 small

8 🎧 2.07 **Listen, find, and say.** They're cats. They're happy.

9 **Make sentences. Say yes or no.**

Number 1. It's a bird. It's ugly.

No. It's beautiful.

Grammar fun!

Grammar: *It's beautiful.* → Workbook page 22

10 🎧 2.08 Sing the song.

I'm at the pet store.
I'm at the pet store.
Can you guess which
pet is my favorite?

Is it small? No, it isn't.
Is it big? Yes, it is.
Is it beautiful? No, it isn't.
Is it ugly? Yes, it is.
It's big and ugly.
Let me guess, let me
guess. Oh, yes!
It's a fish! It's a fish!

I'm at the pet store.
I'm at the pet store.
Can you guess which
pets are my favorites?

Are they old? No, they aren't.
Are they young? Yes, they are.
Are they sad? No, they aren't.
Are they happy? Yes, they are.
They're young and happy.
Let me guess, let me guess. Oh, yes!
They're dogs! They're dogs!

11 Think Play the game.

Is it happy?   No it isn't.

Is it a dog?   Yes, it is!

Are they beautiful?   No, they aren't.

Are they spiders?   Yes, they are!

Grammar: *Is it small?*

Grammar fun!

13   **Listen and act.**

Animal sounds

14 **Listen and say.**

A fox with a fish. A vulture with vegetables.

What do **animals** need?

1 🎧 2.15 Listen and say.

water

food

shelter

2 CLIL ▶ Watch the video.

3 Look and say *water*, *food*, or *shelter*.

Number 1. Water.   Yes!

Guess What!

Let's collaborate!

OUR PET VIDEO

find out
think
choose
film
discuss
agree

Review Units 1 and 2

1 Look and say the words.

Number 1. Bus.

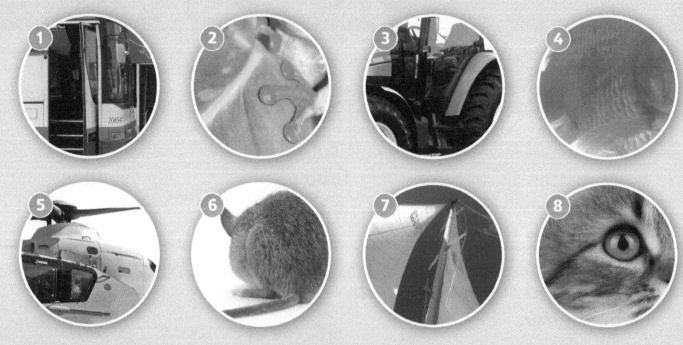

2 🎧 2.16 Listen and say the color.

Tony   Anna   May   Bill

3 Play the game.

What's this? / What are these?	How do you spell … ?	What does he/she have?	Is he / Are they … ?
1	**2**	**3**	**4**

beautiful?

old?

young?

sad?

Look!

Guess What!

theme

8

1 🎧 3.01 **Listen. Who's speaking?**

2 🎧 3.02 **Listen, point, and say.**

THE THEATER
presents

WOOF!

1 jacket

2 pants

3 socks

4 skirt

5 shoes

6 dress

7 T-shirt

8 jeans

9 shirt

3 🎧 3.03 **Listen and find.**

Find Leo

4 (3.04) Say the chant.

red jacket

green T-shirt

purple shoes

blue pants

Here's your jacket,
Your favorite red jacket.
Put on your jacket,
Let's go out and play.

Here are your shoes,
Your favorite purple shoes.
Put on your shoes,
Let's go out and play.

5 Think Find the mistakes and say.

His T-shirt isn't
red. It's yellow.

Her shoes aren't
orange. They're red.

6 🎧 3.06 Sing the song.

What are you wearing?
What are you wearing?
What are you wearing today?

I'm wearing red
And a green .
I'm wearing a blue
And a yellow 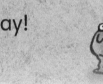 .
Oh! I look great today!

I'm wearing blue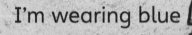
And an orange .
I'm wearing a green
And a purple .
Oh! I look great today!

7 🎧 3.07 Think Listen and say the name.

Sammy

Sally

8 About Me Ask and answer.

What are you wearing today?

I'm wearing a blue skirt.

Grammar fun!

Grammar: *What are you wearing?*

→ Workbook page 32

9 🎧 3.08 **Listen, look, and say.**

1 Are you wearing a blue T-shirt?

Yes, I am.

2 Are you wearing brown shoes?

No, I'm not.

10 🎧 3.09 **Listen and point. Then play the game.**

Pink. Pants.
Are you wearing pink pants?

No, I'm not. My turn!

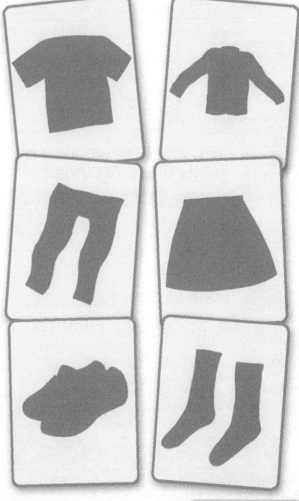

Grammar: *Are you wearing a blue T-shirt?*

Grammar fun!

→ Workbook page 34

12 **Talk Time** **Listen and act.**

Animal sounds

13 🎧 3.14 **Listen and say.**

Jackals don't like jello. Yaks don't like yogurt.

What are
clothes
made of?

1 🎧 3.16 Listen and say.

cotton   silk   leather   wool

2 CLIL ▶ Watch the video.

3 Look and say the material.

Number 1. Wool.   Yes!

1

2

3

4

5

Guess What?

Let's collaborate!

OUR CLOTHES COLLAGE
boots
jacket
agree
hat
create
design

4 Rooms

Look!

Guess What!

theme

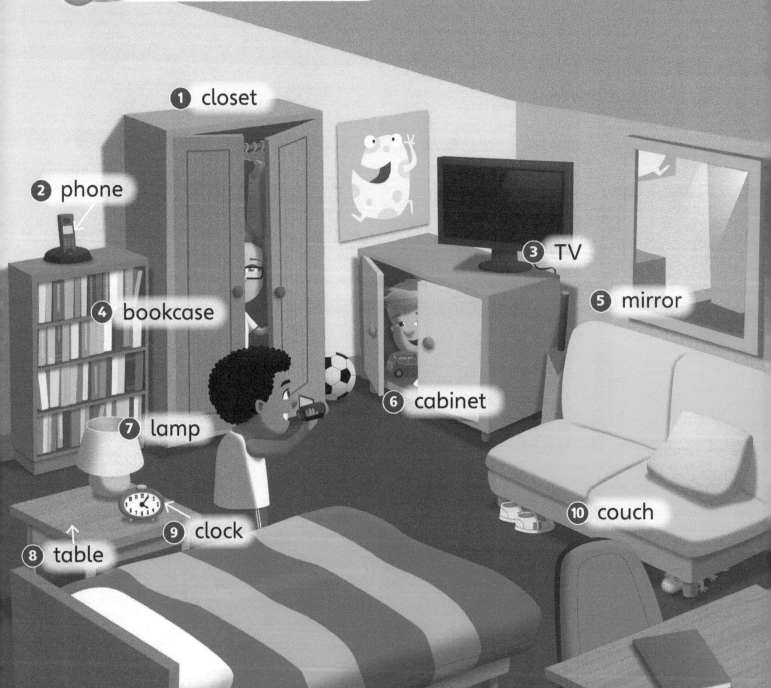

1 closet

2 phone

4 bookcase

3 TV

5 mirror

6 cabinet

7 lamp

9 clock

8 table

10 couch

Find Leo

3 🎧 4.03 **Listen and find.**

Say the chant.

Is the lamp on the table?
Yes, it is. Yes, it is.
The lamp's on the table.

Are the books in the bookcase?
Yes, they are. Yes, they are.
The books are in the bookcase.

lamp

bookcase

clock

closet

  Look, ask, and answer.

Is the phone on the bookcase?

No, it isn't. It's on the table.

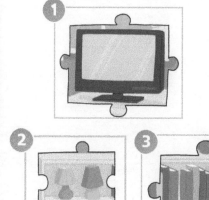

  What's in your bedroom? Think and say.

My computer is on my desk.

It's moving day, it's moving day,
And everything's wrong
on moving day.

There's a  in the bathroom.
There's a in the hallway.
There's a in the kitchen.
And I can't find my ball today!

It's moving day …

There are four s in the yard.
There are two s on my bed.
There are three s on the couch.
And where is baby Fred?

It's moving day …

8 (4.07) **Listen and say *yes* or *no*.**

Grammar: *There's a couch in the bathroom.*   → Workbook page 40

9 4.08 Listen, look, and say.

10 4.09 Listen, count, and answer the questions.

How many fish are there?

Seventeen!

11 Think Play the game.

There are three spiders.

No!

→ Workbook page 41   Grammar: *How many books are there?*

Value: Be neat

→ Workbook page 42

13 (4.12) **Talk Time** **Listen and act.**

Animal sounds

14 (4.13) **Listen and say.**

Meerkats have mouths. Newts have noses.

How many are there?

1 🎧 4.15 Listen and say.

1 streetlight

2 bus stop

3 mailbox

4 traffic light

2 CLIL ▶ Watch the video.

Guess What!

3 Look and say the number.

How many streetlights are there?

There are fourteen.

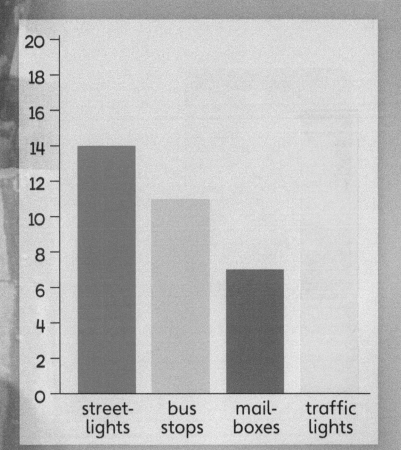

Let's collaborate!

OUR **BAR CHART**
cafeteria
classroom
library
office
count
compare

→ Workbook page 44   CLIL: Math   55

Review Units 3 and 4

1 Look and say the words. | Number 1. Jeans.

2 (4.16) Listen and say the color.

Finish

Are you wearing a
 ?
17

How many

are there in your house?
18

Are you wearing a
?
19

GO BACK ONE!
20

MISS A TURN!
16

How many
are there in your bathroom?
15

Are you wearing a
?
14

How many
are there in your classroom?
13

Are you wearing a
?
9

How many
are there in your kitchen?
10

Are you wearing
?
11

GO BACK ONE!
12

GO FORWARD ONE!
8

How many
are there in your living room?
7

Are you wearing
?
6

How many
are there in your bedroom?
5

Are you wearing
?
1

How many
are there in your classroom?
2

Are you wearing a
?

MISS A TURN!
4

Start

5 Meals

Look!

Guess What!

1 🎧 5.01 Listen. Who's speaking?

2 🎧 5.02 Listen, point, and say.

1 potatoes
2 carrots
3 rice
4 peas
5 sausages
6 fish
7 meat
8 beans
9 toast
10 cereal

The Ca
Breakfast 8-
Lunch 12
Dinner 4

3 🎧 5.03 Listen and find.

Find Leo

4 Say the chant.

breakfast

Do you like toast for breakfast?
Do you like cereal, too?
Toast and cereal for breakfast?
Yum! Yes, I do.

lunch

dinner

5 Think Read, look, and say. What's missing?

Shopping list

cereal

sausages

meat

peas

potatoes

beans

rice

fish

→ Workbook page 49

Vocabulary **61**

6 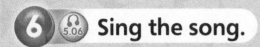 **Sing the song.**

My friend Sammy likes 🍗 for lunch.
He doesn't like 🥔,
And he doesn't like 🫘.
He likes 🫘 and 🥕,
And he likes 🧀.

Munch, Sammy.
Munch your lunch!

My friend Sally likes 🐟 for lunch.
She doesn't like 🧀,
And she doesn't like 🍗.
She likes 🫘 and 🥕,
And 🥔 and 🫘.

Munch, Sally.
Munch your lunch!

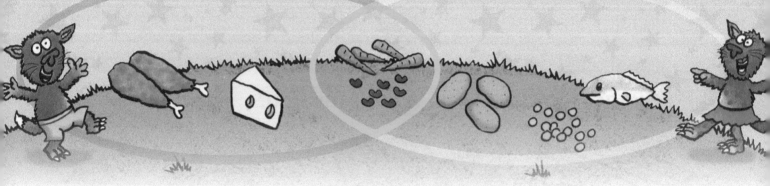

7 **Listen and say *Sammy* or *Sally*.**

8 (About Me) **Ask and answer. Then say.**

Do you like fish?

Yes, I do.

Alex likes fish.

Grammar: *My friend Sammy likes meat for lunch.* → Workbook page 50

9 5.09 Listen, look, and say.

1

2

10 Think Ask and answer.

Tony

Is it a boy or a girl?

It's a boy.

Does he like meat?

Yes, he does.

Does he like carrots?

No, he doesn't.

It's Tony!

Kim

Tom

Pat

→ Workbook page 51

Grammar: *Does he like cereal?*

Grammar fun!

1

Look! Café Hawaii!

Café Hawaii

Let's go for lunch!

2

Café Hawaii

Would you like fish and potatoes?

Yes, please!

No, thank you!

3

What about carrots or peas, iPal?

No, thank you!

4

Oh, dear! What would you like, iPal?

Cake! I like chocolate cake.

5

More cake, please!

No, iPal. That's enough!

6

What's the matter?

He likes chocolate cake – a lot!

64 | **Value:** Eat healthy food

→ Workbook page 52

12 **Listen and act.**

Animal sounds

13 **Listen and say.**

A seal in the sun. A zebra in the zoo.

What kind of **food** is it?

1 🎧 5.15 Listen and say.

fruit vegetables meat grains dairy

2 CLIL ▶ Watch the video.

Guess What?

3 Look and say what kind of food it is.

Number 1. Fish.   Yes.

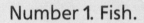

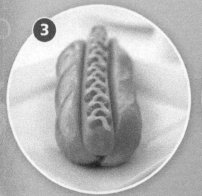

Let's collaborate!

OUR NEW
HEALTHY CAFÉ MENU

lunch discuss dinner
breakfast present
create

6 Activities

Look!

Guess What!

69

1 🎧 6.01 **Listen. Who's speaking?**

2 🎧 6.02 **Listen, point, and say.**

Activity Day what can you do?

1 play tennis
2 play field hockey
3 play basketball
4 roller-skate
5 play baseball
6 ride a horse
7 fly a kite
8 take photographs

TODAY!

Find Leo

3 🎧 6.03 **Listen and find.**

4 Say the chant.

I can play tennis.
I can't play field hockey.
Let's play tennis.
Good idea!

basketball
baseball

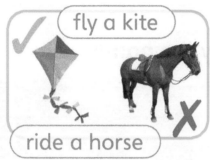
fly a kite
ride a horse

take photographs
roller-skate

5 Match and say.

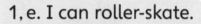 1, e. I can roller-skate.

1 I can roller-skate.
2 I can take photographs.
3 I can ride a horse.
4 I can play tennis.
5 I can play field hockey.

a

b

c

d

e

6 Point and tell your friend.

Picture b. I can play tennis.

Picture e. I can't roller-skate.

→ Workbook page 57

Vocabulary **71**

7 **Listen, look, and say.**

1. I like playing basketball, I don't like swimming.

2. I like swimming. I don't like playing basketball.

8 **Listen and say the name.**

Ann

Pam

Jack

Bill

Alex

Grace

9 **Things you like. Think and say.**

I like painting.   He likes painting.

72

10 🎧 6.08 Sing the song.

Do you like ?
No, I don't. No, I don't.
Do you like ?
Yes, I do. Yes, I do.
I like !

Does he like ?
No, he doesn't. No, he doesn't.
Does he like ?
Yes, he does. Yes, he does.
He likes !

Do you like ?
No, I don't. No, I don't.
Do you like ?
Yes, I do. Yes, I do.
I like !

Does she like ?
No, she doesn't. No, she doesn't.
Does she like ?
Yes, she does. Yes, she does.
She likes !

11 🎧 6.09 Think Listen and say the number.

1
2
3
4
5
6

→ Workbook page 59   Grammar: *Do you like flying a kite?*

Grammar fun!

1
It's a basketball!

Are you OK, David?

2
The All Stars are my favorite team!

Let's play! Put on these shirts!

3
HOME 25 GUEST 25

That's not fair!

Play nicely, iPal.

4
I'm sorry.

That's OK.

5
HOME 25 GUEST 25

Watch me! Throw the ball like this.

Yes!

74 Value: Play nicely

6
HOME 27 GUEST 25

Good job, Olivia!

Thanks, iPal.

→ Workbook page 60

13 **Talk Time** 6.12 **Listen and act.**

Animal sounds

14 6.13 **Listen and say.**

**A camel with
a camera.
A kangaroo
with a kite.**

What equipment do we need?

1 🎧 6.15 **Listen and say.**

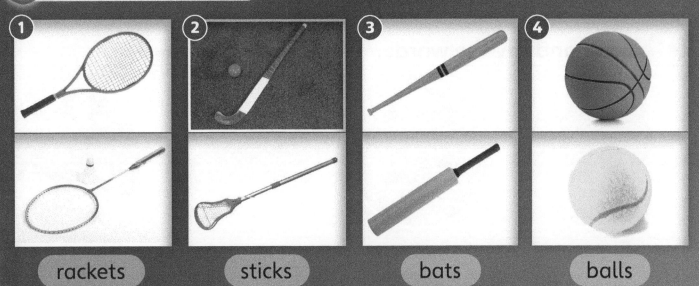

rackets   sticks   bats   balls

2 CLIL ▶ **Watch the video.**

3 **Look and say** *racket,* *stick, bat,* or *ball.*

Number 1. Ball.   Yes!

Guess What!

Let's collaborate!

actions   agree   present   LET'S EXPLAIN A GAME   body parts   team   find out

Review Units 5 and 6

1 Look and say the words.

Number 1. Fly a kite.

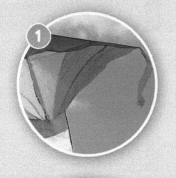

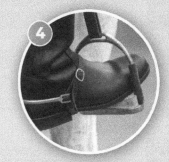

2 🎧 6.16 Listen and say the color.

Sue

Dan

→ Workbook pages 64–65

3 **Play the game.**

Do you like ?

Does he like ?

18 Do you like ?

Finish

15 Does she like ?

14 Do you like ?

13 Does he like ?

12 Do you like ?

8 Do you like ?

Does he like ?

9 Do you like ?

Does she like ?

11

10

7 Does she like ?

6 Do you like ?

Does he like ?

5 Does he like ?

4 Do you like ?

3 Does she like ?

Start

1 Does he like ?

2 Do you like ?

79

7 In town

Look!

Guess What!

1 (7.01) Listen. Who's speaking?

2 (7.02) Listen, point, and say.

1 park

2 movie theater

3 clothing store

4 café

5 toy store

6 bookstore

7 supermarket

8 street

9 school

10 playground

3 (7.03) Listen and find.

Find Leo

4 **Say the chant.**

Come with me and look around.
Who's in the café in the town?
It's my sister! She's in the café.
She's in the café in the town.

sister

brother   mom

dad

5 **Match and say.**

1, c. My cousin's on the playground.

1 My cousin's on the playground.
2 My aunt's in the clothing store.
3 My uncle's in the school.
4 My grandma's in the supermarket.
5 My grandpa's at the park.

6 **Think of a place. Say and guess.**

There's a desk and green chairs.

It's a school.

→ Workbook page 67   Vocabulary **83**

7 🎧 (7.06) **Sing the song.**

Come and visit my town,
My friendly little town.
It's nice to be in my town,
My little town.

There's a toy store and
a clothing store.
There's a bookstore
and a movie theater.
There's a café, and
there's a supermarket.
In my little town.

And the toy store is behind the
clothing store.
And the bookstore is in front of
the clothing store.
And the clothing store is between
the bookstore and the toy store!
In my little town.

And the movie theater is next to the café.
And the café is next to the supermarket.
And the café is between the supermarket
and the movie theater.

Come and visit my town …

8 🎧 (7.07) **Look, listen, and find the mistakes.**

> The movie theater is next to the supermarket.

> No, it isn't. The movie theater is next to the café.

Grammar: *The toy store is behind the clothing store.* → Workbook page 68

9 **Listen, look, and say.**

Is there a playground behind the school?

Yes, there is.

Is there a café next to the movie theater?

No, there isn't.

10 **Listen and say *yes* or *no*.**

11 **Play the game.**

Is there a café in front of the supermarket?

Yes, there is.

The movie theater is next to the school.

No, it isn't. The movie theater is next to the supermarket.

→ Workbook page 69   Grammar: *Is there a playground behind the school?*

 Grammar fun!

13   **Listen and act.**

Animal sounds

14 🎧 7.13 **Listen and say.**

A quick queen bee. An ox with an X-ray.

Where are the
places?

1 🎧 7.15 Listen and say.

police station | fire station | hospital | sports center

2 CLIL ▶ Watch the video.

3 Look and say the letter and number.

A, 3. | Fire station. | Yes!

Guess What!

Let's collaborate!

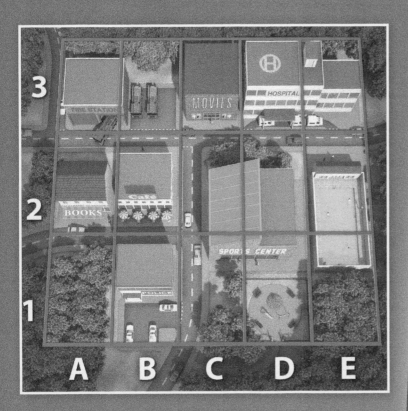

3 2 1 — A B C D E

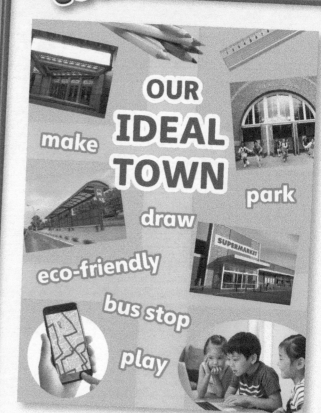

make **OUR IDEAL TOWN** park draw eco-friendly bus stop play

8 On the farm

Look!

▶

Guess What!

1 🎧 8.01 **Listen. Who's speaking?**

2 🎧 8.02 **Listen, point, and say.**

Café and Gift Store

1 field

2 barn

3 horse

4 donkey

5 sheep

6 goat

7 cow

8 duck

3 🎧 8.03 **Listen and find.**

9 pond

Find Leo

Say the chant.

donkey

Where's the donkey?
It's in the barn.
It's in the barn.
On the farm.

Where are the goats?
They're in the field.
They're in the field.
On the farm.

cow

goats

ducks

5 **Read and follow. Then ask and answer.**

Where's the cow? It's in the field.

1 Where's the cow?

2 Where are the ducks?

3 Where are the sheep?

4 Where's the horse?

 a

 b

c

6 Ask and answer.

What's your favorite animal? It's a sheep.

7 🎧 8.06 Sing the song.

Field and pond, house and barn,

Look at the animals on the farm …

What's the 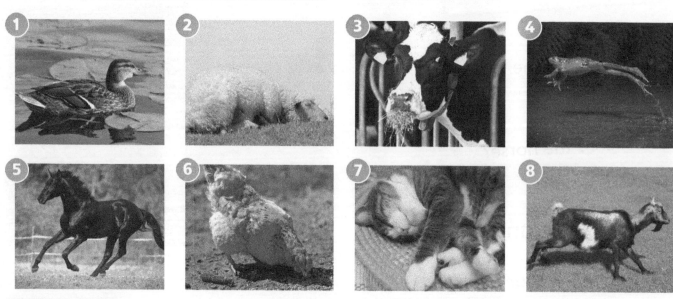 doing?

It's swimming. It's swimming.

It's swimming.

What's the doing?

It's swimming in the .

Field and pond …

What's the doing?

It's running. It's running. It's running.

What's the doing?

It's running in the .

Field and pond …

What's the doing?

It's sleeping. It's sleeping.

It's sleeping.

What's the doing?

It's sleeping in the .

Field and pond …

What's the doing?

It's eating. It's eating. It's eating.

What's the doing?

It's eating in the .

Field and pond …

8 🎧 8.07 Listen and answer the questions.

What's the duck doing?   It's swimming.

Grammar: *What's the duck doing?*   → Workbook page 76

9 🎧 8.08 Listen, look, and say.

1 Is the cat sleeping?   Yes, it is.

2 Is the duck swimming?   No, it isn't. It's flying.

10 Think Play the game.

Is the dog running?   Yes, it is.

Picture 1!

→ Workbook page 77   Grammar: *Is the cat sleeping?*   Grammar fun!

1 It's a message for iPal.

Let's find him!

2 Would you like to come to a party?

Yes, please!

3 Hold on!

We're flying!

4 Welcome to the party!

It's so nice to see you!

WELCOME HOME

5 What's Ben doing?

He's ... dancing!

6 Goodbye, iPal!

Goodbye! Thanks for taking care of me!

96 Value: Love your home

→ Workbook page 78

12   **Listen and act.**

Animal sounds

13  **Listen and say.**

A **wolf** in
the **water**.
A **white whale**
with a **wheel**.

Functional language: *Would you like to come to my party?*
Pronunciation: *w, wh* **97**

What do **farmers** do?

1 🎧 8.15 Listen and say.

1 plant seeds

2 turn soil

3 water plants

4 harvest plants

2 CLIL ▶ Watch the video.

3 Look and say.

Number 1. He turns soil.   Yes!

1

2

3

4

Guess What!

Let's collaborate!

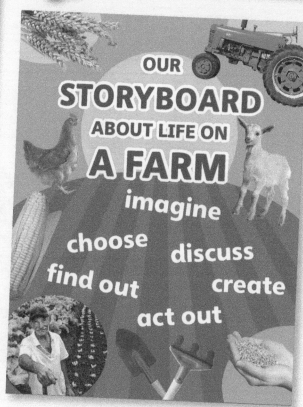

OUR **STORYBOARD** ABOUT LIFE ON **A FARM**

imagine

choose   discuss

find out   create

act out

→ Workbook page 80   CLIL: Science

Review Units 7 and 8

1 Look and say the words.

Number 1. Café.

2 🎧 8.16 Listen and say the name.

Grace

Lola

Kento

Dan

3 Ask and answer.

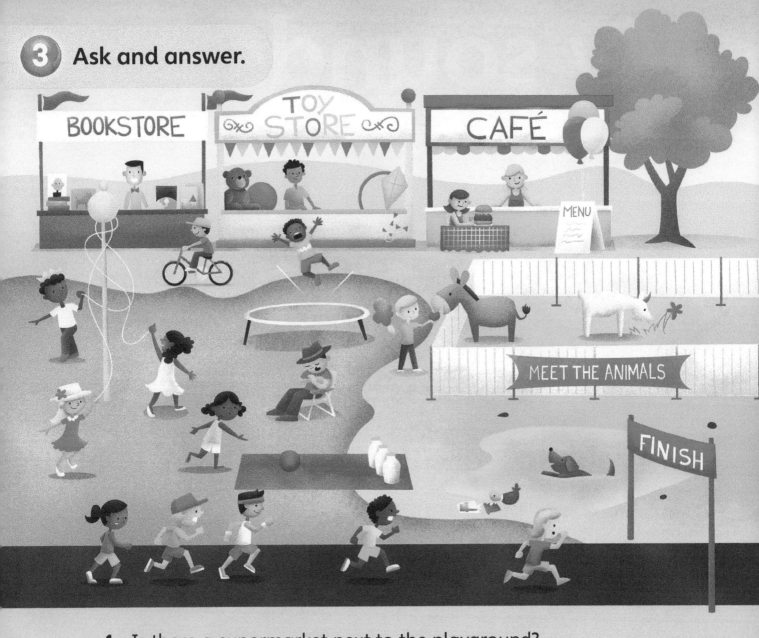

1 Is there a supermarket next to the playground?

2 What is between the bookstore and the café?

3 Is there a pond at the park?

4 What is the duck doing?

5 Is the dog sleeping?

6 What is the donkey doing?

7 Is she eating cereal?

8 What's he doing?

9 Is she swimming?

10 What's he doing?

My sounds

lion • rabbit

gorilla • hippo

fox • vulture

jackal • yak

meerkat • newt

seal • zebra

camel • kangaroo

queen bee • ox

wolf • whale

Acknowledgments

Many thanks to everyone in the excellent team at Cambridge University Press & Assessment in Spain, the UK, and India.

The authors and publishers would like to thank the following contributors:
Blooberry Design: concept design, cover design, book design
Hyphen: publishing management, page make-up
Ann Thomson: art direction
Gareth Boden: commissioned photography
Jon Barlow: commissioned photography
Ian Harker: class audio recording
John Marshall Media: "Grammar fun" recordings
Robert Lee, Dib Dib Dub Studios: song and chant composition
Vince Cross: theme tune composition
James Richardson: arrangement of theme tune
Phaebus: "CLIL" video production
Kiki Foster: "Look!" video production
Bill Smith Group: "Grammar fun" and story animations
Sounds Like Mike Ltd: "Grammar Fun" video production

The authors and publishers acknowledge the following sources of copyright material and are grateful for the permissions granted. Although every effort has been made, it has not always been possible to identify the sources of all the material used or to trace all copyright holders. If any omissions are brought to our notice, we will be happy to include the appropriate acknowledgments on reprinting and in the next update to the digital edition, as applicable.

Key: U = Unit.

Photography

The following photos are sourced from Getty Images:
U0: Ariel Skelley/DigitalVision; enjoynz/DigitalVision Vectors; Corbis; enjoynz/DigitalVision Vectors; Sappington Todd/BLOOMimage; Burazin/The Image Bank; VISIT ROEMVANITCH; Burazin; Lane Oatey/Blue Jean Images; Lane Oatey/Blue Jean images/blue jean images; Sappington Todd; aire images/Moment; Andrew Bret Wallis/Photodisc; Visit Roemvanitch/EyeEm; U1: Ayhan Altun/Moment; Aargentieri/iStock Getty Images Plus; szefei/iStock/Getty Images Plus; alxpin/E+; Henrik5000/E+; Spondylolithesis/E+; Klaus Vedfelt/DigitalVision; SteveDF/E+;CHUYN/DigitalVision Vectors; alxpin/E+; U2: antos777/iStock/Getty Images Plus; BarbarosKARAGULMEZ/iStock/Getty Images Plus; Aargentieri/iStock/Getty Images Plus; Lawrence Manning/Corbis; kgfoto/E+; Nophamon Yanyapong/EyeEm; Lew Robertson/Stone; Lényfotó pet photography/500px; RF Pictures/The Image Bank; Hans Surfer/Moment; Oscar Wong/Moment; Lucas Ninno/Moment; mehmettorlak/E+; dszc/E+; U3: hadynyah/E+; Emilia Drewniak/EyeEm; fotograzia/Moment; Santiago Urquijo/Moment; Sittichai Karimpard/EyeEm; Eduardo Lopez Coronado/EyeEm; Burazin/The Image Bank; Peter Dazeley/The Image Bank; Rawin Tanpin/EyeEm; Anatoliy Sadovskiy/EyeEm; mikroman6/Moment; kelly bowden/Moment; iStock/Getty Images; Eduardo1961/iStock; mikroman6/Getty images; Anatoliy Sadovskiy/EyeEm; U4: LeeYiuTung/iStock/Getty Images Plus; LianeM/iStock/Getty Images Plus; Lew Robertson/Corbis; SDI Productions/E+; pepifoto/E+; Waridsara Pitakpon/EyeEm; Russ Witherington/EyeEm; Rizki Wanggono/EyeEm; U5: Andrew Olney/Stockbyte; Adam Gault/OJO Images; bluehill75/E+; Mohd Haniff Abas/EyeEm; Stockbyte; FatCamera/E+; John A. Rizzo/Photodisc; Juanmonino/E+; AdShooter/E+; Mohd Haniff Abas /EyeEm; Stockbyte/Stockbyte; U6: Leander Baerenz/Getty Images ; Hybrid Images/Getty Images; Lauri Patterson/Getty Images; Image Source; Glyn Jones/Corbis/VCG; Yevgen Romanenko/Moment; Lawrence Manning/Corbis; Blake Little/Stone; George Doyle/Stockbyte; Photodisc; U7: lucentius/iStock/Getty Images Plus; Andersen Ross Photography Inc/DigitalVision/Getty images; AlexSava/E+; Marje/E+; Poh Kim Yeoh/EyeEm; MirageC/Moment; David Zaitz/The Image Bank Unreleased; Andersen Ross Photography Inc/DigitalVision; 500px Asia; LordRunar/E+; Nipitphon Na Chiangmai/EyeEm; Nipitphon Na Chiangmai/EyeEm; U8: BlazenImages/iStock/Getty Images Plus; Stephen Dorey/Getty Images; SCIENCE PHOTO LIBRARY; kickstand/E+; Burazin/The Image Bank; Life On White/Photodisc; Supawat Punnanon/EyeEm; Igor Alecsander/E+; Theerasak Tammachuen/EyeEm; Floortje/E+; Image Source.

The following photos are sourced from other libraries:
U0: VALUA VITALY; Jacek Chabraszewski; Monkey Business Images; BNP Design Studio; michaeljung; Anna Andersson Fotografi; terekhov igor; Wil Tilroe-Otte; Gena73; incamerastock/Alamy Stock Photo; Zoonar GmbH/Alamy Stock Photo; Robin Weaver/Alamy Stock Photo; REDPIXEL.PL; Yeamake; veryan dale/Alamy Stock Photo; Africa Studio/Shutterstock; Serge Vero/Shutterstock; Matej

Kastelic; MaKars/Shutterstock; U1: Philip Lange/Shutterstock; Margo Harrison; John Orsbun; Margo Harrison; James Steidl; Scott Rothstein; one pony; s_oleg; Aprilphoto; Mikael Damkier; imageBROKER.com GmbH & Co. KG/ Alamy Stock Photo; Buzz Pictures/Alamy; antb/Shutterstock ; Dhoxax/Shutterstock; Bailey-Cooper Photography/Alamy Stock Photo; David Fowler; Dwight Smith; Andrey Pavlov; Elena Elisseeva; Patrick Foto; maxpro; U2: Viorel Sima; stockyimages; StockLite; Gelpi; SurangaSL/Shutterstock; Barna Tanko; g215; Tierfotoagentur/Alamy; J Reineke; skynetphoto; Galyna Andrushko; Don Fink; Vitaly Titov; shane partdridge/Alamy; Mikael Damkier/Shutterstock; paul prescott/Shutterstock; Tsekhmister/Shutterstock; Olga Bogatyrenko/Shutterstock; DenisNata/Shutterstock; MANDY GODBEHEAR/Shutterstock; Judy Kennamer/Shutterstock; Monkey Business Images/Shutterstock; Willyam Bradberry/Shutterstock; Matthew Williams-Ellis/Shutterstock; Geoffrey Lawrence/Shutterstock; DreamBig/Shutterstock; U3: Mo Peerbacus/Alamy Stock Photo; Zoonar GmbH/Alamy; artproem/Shutterstock; Irina Rogova/Shutterstock; Tim Gainey/Alamy Stock Photo; Sofiaworld/Shutterstock; smereka/Shutterstock; Randy Rimland/Shutterstock; pixbox77/Shutterstock; Tramont_ana/Shutterstock; Derya Cakirsoy/Shutterstock; trossofoto/Shutterstock; Anna Klepatckaya/Shutterstock; Picsfive/Shutterstock; karkas/Shutterstock; Gulgun Ozaktas/Shutterstock; Loskutnikov/Shutterstock; U4: donatas1205/Shutterstock; akud/Shutterstock; Image navi - QxQ images/Alamy Stock Photo; Justin Kase zsixz/Alamy; Design Pics/Alamy Stock Photo; Taina Sohlman/Shutterstock; stocker1970/Shutterstock; Teerasak/Shutterstock; Kitch Bain/Shutterstock; Marek Ariel Skelley/DigitalVision Uszynski/Alamy; PearlBucknall/Alamy Stock Photo; Africa Studio/Shutterstock; Yeamake/Shutterstock; Nolte Lourens/Shutterstock; Image Source/Alamy; U5: Naho Yoshizawa/Shutterstock; Craig Richardson/Alamy; Tracy Whiteside/Alamy; Tetra Images,LLC/Alamy; Tracy Whiteside/Alamy; Stefano Politi Markovina/Alamy Stock Photo; matka_Wariatka/Shutterstock; Kolpakova Svetlana/Shutterstock; Jag_cz/Shutterstock; Christine Langer-Pueschel/Shutterstock; Christian Draghici/Shutterstock; koss13/Shutterstock; Christian Jung/Shutterstock; Africa Studio/Shutterstock; U6: Dan Thornberg/Shutterstock; Krakenimages.com/Shutterstock; Hurst Photo/Shutterstock; Alex White/Shutterstock; taelove7/Shutterstock; J.Helgason/Shutterstock; gorillaimages/Shutterstock; Veronica Louro/Shutterstock; Ramona Heim/Shutterstock; Rob Bouwman/Shutterstock; J. Helgason/Shutterstock; Production Perig/Shutterstock; Production Perig/Shutterstock; Phovoir/Shutterstock; ESB Professional/Shutterstock; Kuttig - People/Alamy; F1online digitale Bildagentur GmbH/Alamy; David Madison/DigitalVision; pukach/Shutterstock; anaken2012/Shutterstock; Image Source Plus/Alamy; Thyrymn2/Alamy; onilmilk/Shutterstock; Sean Gladwell/Shutterstock; Aaron Amat/Shutterstock; mexrix/Shutterstock; Pal2iyawit/Shutterstock; Ledo/Shutterstock; Nattika/Shutterstock; Ramon grosso dolarea/Shutterstock; Lotus_studio/Shutterstock; Bits And Splits/Shutterstock; Joe Gough/Shutterstock; Elnur/Shutterstock; Tracy Whiteside/Shutterstock; oliveromg/Shutterstock; Igor Dutina/Shutterstock; StockPhotosArt/Shutterstock; Leonid Shcheglov/Shutterstock.; U7: Gladskikh Tatiana/Shutterstock; Pavel L Photo and Video/Shutterstock; stockfour/Shutterstock; Carlos Yudica/Shutterstock; Brett Baunton/Alamy; A.P.S.(UK)/Alamy; meunierd/Shutterstock; Mike Robinson/Alamy; U8: Dieter Hawlan/Shutterstock; Orhan Cam/Shutterstock; Sebastian Knight/Shutterstock; Luca Santilli/Shutterstock; Joseph Sohm/Shutterstock; Scott Prokop/Shutterstock; BrianGoodman/Shutterstock; Diane Picard/Shutterstock; Schubbel/Shutterstock; Ewa Studio/Shutterstock; Makarova Viktoria/Shutterstock; Kemeo/Shutterstock; val lawless/Shutterstock; Alexander Matvienko/Alamy; Jolanta Wojcicka/Shutterstock; Danylo Saniylenko/Shutterstock; Tim Scrivener/Alamy; Keith Dannemiller/Corbis; Alex Treadway/National Geographic Society/Corbis; Tim Scrivener/Alamy Stock Photo; Arterra Picture Library/Alamy; THP Creative/Shutterstock; Brandon Seidel/Shutterstock; 1stGallery/Shutterstock; Denise Lett/Shutterstock; imageBROKER/Alamy; IxMaster/Shutterstock; Tetra Images/Alamy Stock Photo; Alinute Silzeviciute/Shutterstock; imageBROKER.com GmbH & Co. KG/Alamy Stock Photo

Front Cover Photography

Front Cover Photo by Arthur Morris/Corbis Documentary.

Illustrations

Aphik; Andy Parker; Bill Bolton; Chris Jevons (Bright Agency); Joelle Dreidemy (Bright Agency); Gareth Conway; Kirsten Collier (Bright Agency); Marcus Cutler (Sylvie Poggio); Marek Jagucki; Phil Garner (Beehive Illustration); Richard Watson (Bright Agency); Woody Fox (Bright Agency).